50

incredible facts
about
OCEANS

by Gloria Barnett

Footprint to the Future

contents

Earth and Oceans — 1

Exploring the Oceans — 5

Physical Conditions — 13

Scuba Diving — 28

Ocean Environments — 35

Why we need Healthy Oceans — 44

Fact

1

Earth is often called the Blue Planet.

Blue is the colour of the water in the oceans. Seawater covers roughly 360,000,000 km² of Earth's surface area.

Fact

②

There are five oceans on planet Earth: the Pacific, Atlantic, Indian, Southern/Antarctic, and Arctic.

You can't see a difference in the water between one named ocean and another. All together these oceans are known by scientists as the World Ocean.

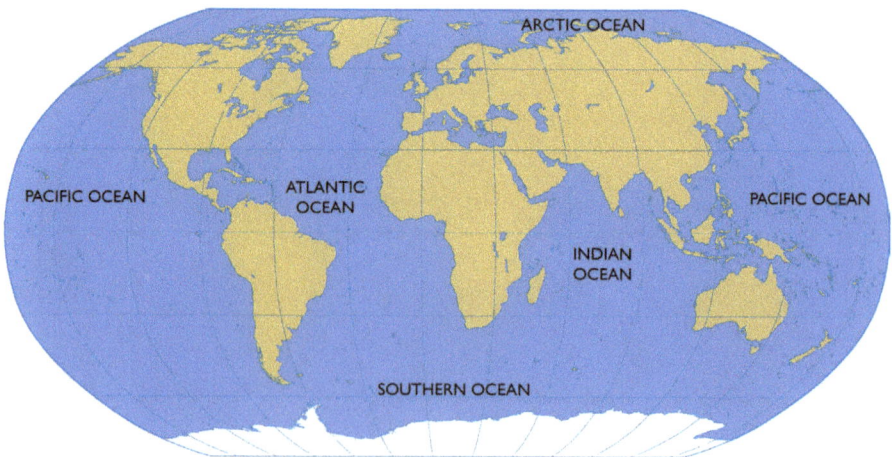

ARCTIC OCEAN

PACIFIC OCEAN

ATLANTIC OCEAN

PACIFIC OCEAN

INDIAN OCEAN

SOUTHERN OCEAN

Fact

③

It is estimated that 70% of the Earth's surface is covered in water.

The Pacific Ocean is the largest ocean on Earth, covering almost half of the Earth's surface – a staggering 46%!

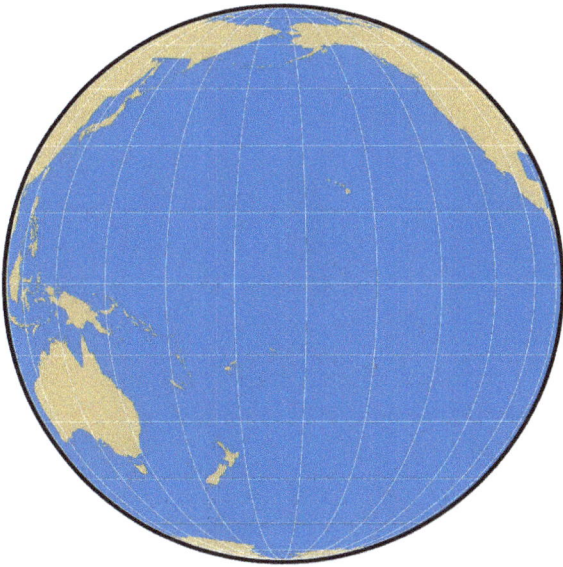

Fact
4

What is the difference between 'oceans' and 'seas'.

Oceans are large bodies of water around the planet. Seas are smaller bodies of water that are part of an ocean. For example, the Mediterranean and the Caribbean Seas are located within the Atlantic Ocean.

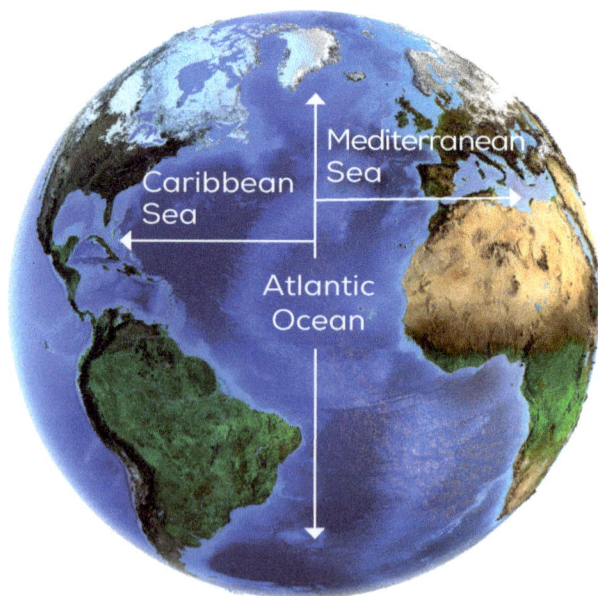

Fact

⑤

The first scientific exploration of the oceans began in 1872 with the ship HMS Challenger.

We have only explored 5% of the Earth's ocean.

Fact
6

We have sent more astronauts to the moon than explorers to the bottom of the ocean.

Humans have travelled further to explore the moon, at over 384 thousand kilometres away, than we have travelled the 11 kilometres to the deepest part of the World Ocean.

Fact

7

Trenches are formed on the crust of the Earth, both on land or deep below the surface of the ocean.

Trenches form when two tectonic plates collide, and one slides beneath the other at a subduction zone.

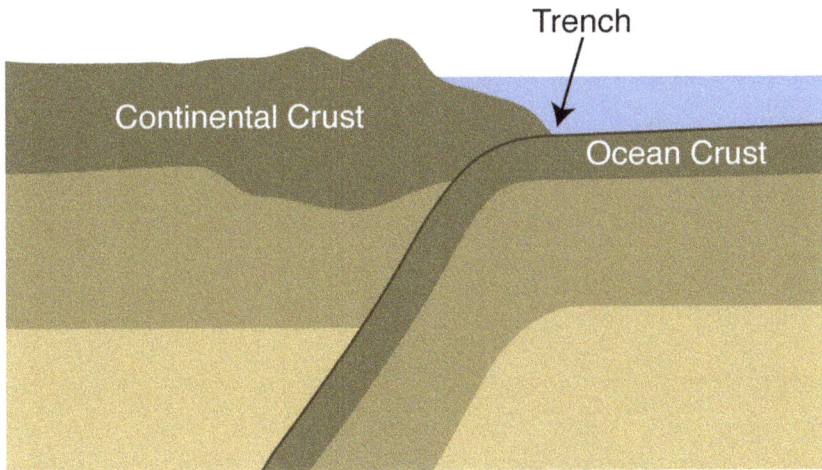

Trench

Continental Crust

Ocean Crust

Fact

8

The deepest part of the World Ocean (11 km down) is the Mariana Trench in the Pacific.

The Pacific Ocean is home to more underwater tectonic plate boundaries than any other place on Earth. The vast number of earthquakes and volcanic eruptions that occur along the rim surrounding the Pacific Ocean is known as the Ring of Fire.

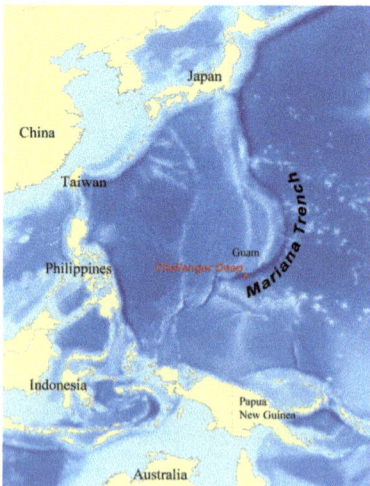

Fact
9

The first manned exploration to the deepest part of the oceans was in 1960.

There was no way these explorers could have been rescued had there been an accident.

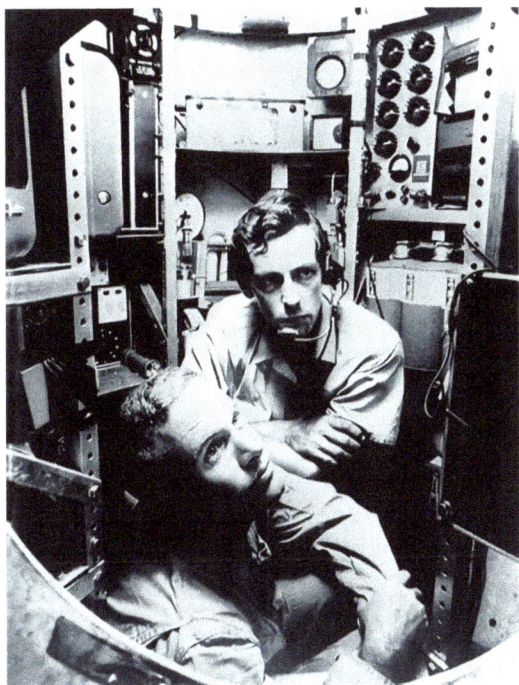

Fact

⑩

In 1960, Don Walsh (USA) and Jacques Piccard (Switzerland) reached the bottom of the Mariana Trench in the bathyscaphe 'Trieste'.

During the descent of 'Trieste', one of the outer windows cracked, but the crew demonstrated their bravery by continuing with the dive instead of immediately returning to the surface.

Fact

11

It was another 50 years before another human travelled to the bottom of the Mariana Trench.

This was James Cameron, the film producer who is famous for making the film 'Titanic'. He travelled to the deepest part of the ocean alone in 2010.

Fact

12

High-tech submersibles are used by ocean explorers to reach the deepest depths of the ocean.

Explorer Viktor Vescova travelled to the deepest parts of all five oceans in the submersible 'Limiting Factor' during 2018-2019.

Fact
13

Salty ocean water contains dissolved mineral salts.

Ocean water contains sodium chloride – the sort of salt you put on your chips. It is poisonous to drink salty sea water.

Fact

14

Sea water contains different chemicals which make it taste 'salty'.

Rainwater is fresh water. Ocean water is salty as it contains chemicals such as sodium, magnesium chlorine, sulphur and potassium.

Fact

⓯

Vast stores of nutrients are brought to the ocean surface by a vertical movement of water called 'upwelling'. This brings a source of food from the depths of the oceans to the surface.

The nutrients which come from the deep, act like fertiliser and help plankton and seaweed to grow.

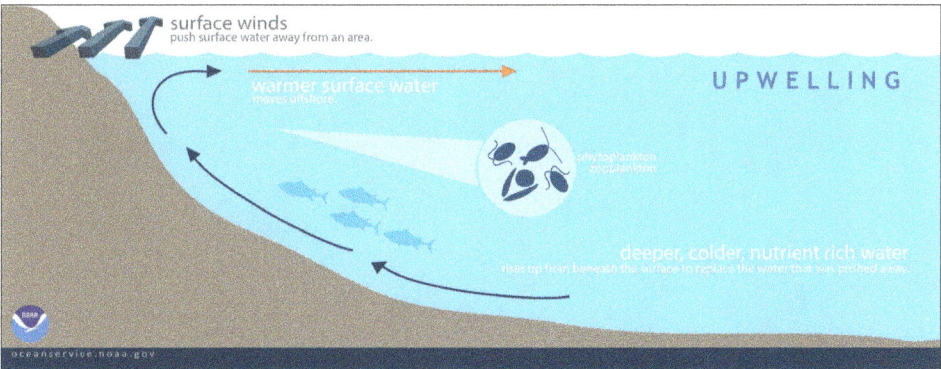

surface winds
push surface water away from an area.

warmer surface water
moves offshore.

UPWELLING

phytoplankton
zooplankton

deeper, colder, nutrient rich water
rises up from beneath the surface to replace the water that was pushed away.

oceanservice.noaa.gov

Fact

16

Water is a limited resource on our planet, with 97.5% being salty water in the oceans.
Only 2.5% of water on Earth has no salt and is fresh water.

Most of the world's freshwater is frozen in Antarctica and Greenland, while the remaining freshwater exists in rivers, lakes, and groundwater. The water cycle ensures that water is recycled and redistributed around the planet.

Fact

17

97% of all freshwater is produced from rain originating from ocean water. The remaining 2.5% of fresh water is stored in glaciers, lakes and rivers on land.

Freshwater is crucial for a healthy life. One in nine people live without access to freshwater. Drinking contaminated water leads to the spread of fatal diseases.

Fact

18

The Water Cycle produces fresh water.

When the sun **heats the ocean, droplets of water evaporate** from the ocean, turning into the gases hydrogen and oxygen (H_2O). These gases **rise to the upper atmosphere to form clouds**. These clouds move around the atmosphere until they cool, and the gases form water droplets, which fall **as raindrops onto land** (precipitation). Fresh **rainwater travels over land**, and humans use it for various purposes such as agriculture and drinking water before **rivers carry the rainwater back to the ocean**, where the cycle starts again.

Fact

19

On land, humans breathe in oxygen in order to live. The air in the atmosphere contains 20% oxygen.

When we are underwater, humans are unable to extract the 1% oxygen dissolved in the water. Fish, however, have evolved gills instead of lungs which enables them to absorb the oxygen in water into their blood stream.

Fact

20

Sunlight becomes dimmer when it hits the surface of water. Water separates the colours of light, causing red to disappear first.

Colours fade as you dive into deep waters, starting from red and ending in black and white at around 25 metres.
Filmmakers use waterproof lights to capture the beauty of the corals and animals living in these depths.

COLOURS ARE LOST AT THESE DEPTHS

0.2m	1m	5m	15m	20m
Red	Orange	Yellow	Green	Blue

Fact

㉑

The Sun provides the Oceans with heat and light.

The Sun is 150 million km away from Earth. The Sun's surface is 5,537°C, and the core is 15 million °C. All the heat energy that reaches the Earth comes from the Sun. It takes 8 minutes for the light to travel from the Sun to Earth. The ocean absorbs the heat and stores it, acting as a heat reservoir.

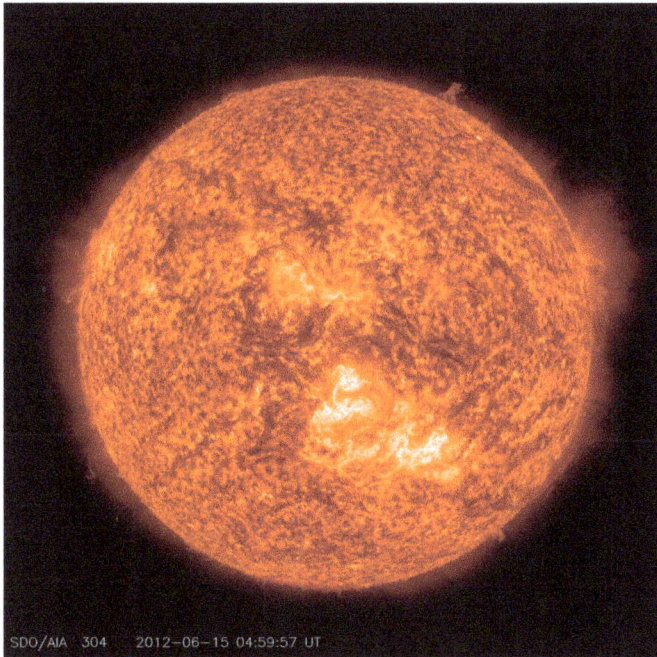

SDO/AIA 304   2012-06-15 04:59:57 UT

Fact

22

The Earth's shape is not a perfect sphere. It bulges around the equator, making the equator closer to the sun and hotter than the polar areas.

The ocean holds heat better than land and currents distribute it globally. Warm currents carry warm water from the equator to the poles, while cold currents take cold water from the poles to the equator.

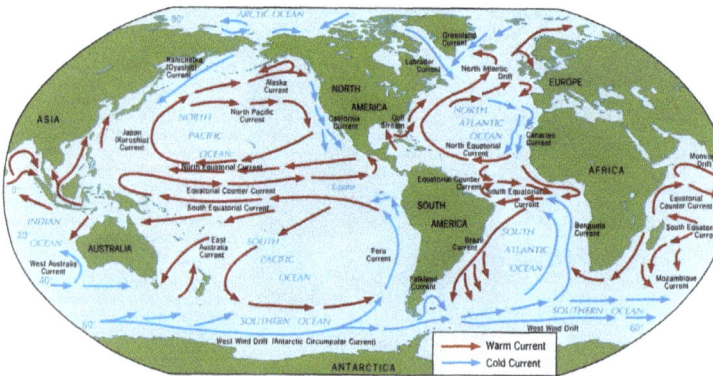

World distribution of ocean currents

Fact
23

A large amount of pressure is created by the vast quantity of water in the oceans. Oceans have very high pressure which increases as you go deeper.

The pressure of the water against your body increases as you go deeper in the water.
Human bodies cannot survive in extreme pressure.

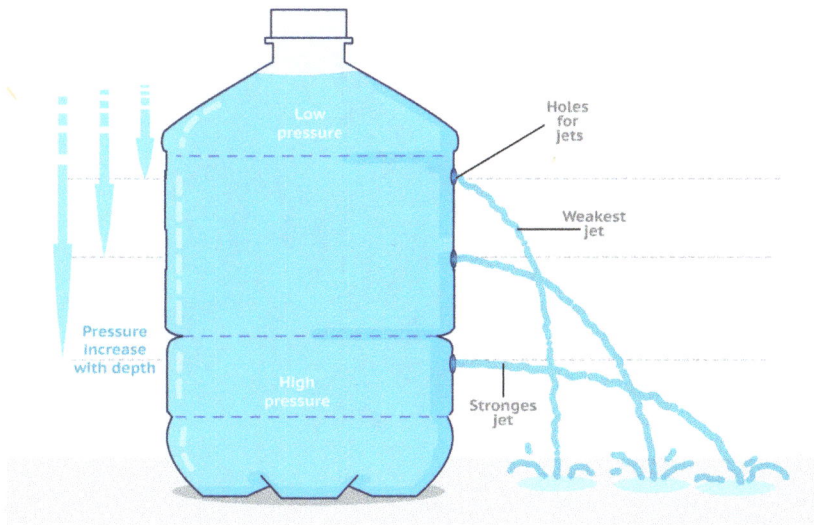

Fact

24

This diagram shows the underwater profile of the oceans. The Earth's crust is not uniform, and the ocean fills the hollows of the crust around the world.

Ocean temperature never drops below 2-3°C. Most living creatures (biomass) live in the top 200m. Oxygen levels get lower the deeper you go. Sunlight doesn't reach below 200m, resulting in the deep ocean environment being in complete darkness.

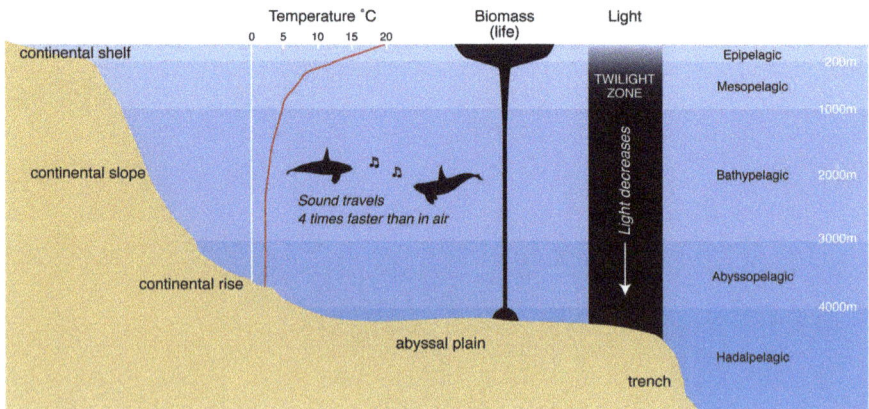

Fact
25

Below the 'Twilight Zone' you enter a complete pitch blackness where no light reaches.

Strange creatures live in this black abyss only seen by humans in the photographs taken from submersibles.

Fact

26

Bioluminescence is a chemical reaction which produces light in some living organisms. Tiny algae drift in the ocean at night, and their bioluminescence cause the surface of the water to sparkle.

Marine creatures living in the dark regions of the ocean use bioluminescence to protect themselves from predators, attract food, or find a mate.

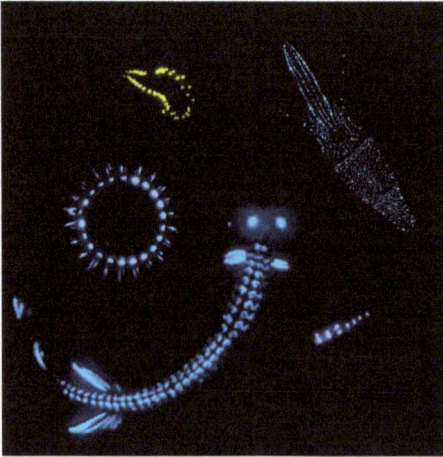

Fact
27

The topmost layer of the ocean, which is called the epipelagic zone, extends from the surface down to a depth of 200 metres. This area is a thriving hub of marine life due to the abundance of sunlight, warmth, and oxygen it receives.

Most living creatures on Earth need oxygen to survive. This is why the majority of fish, reptiles, and marine mammals prefer to live in the upper 200 metres of the ocean. The epipelagic zone is home to a large variety of animals such as plankton, invertebrates, fish, reptiles, and marine mammals.

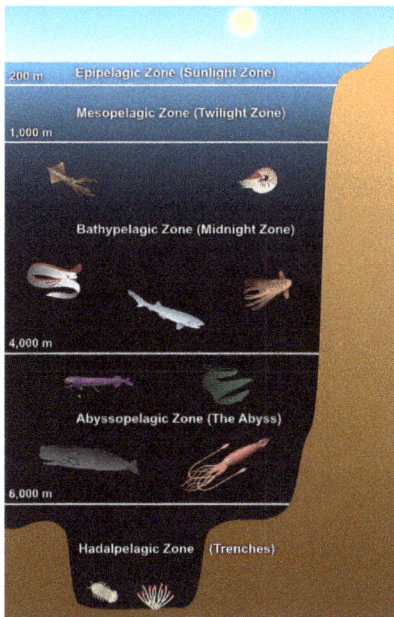

Fact
28

Scuba, which stands for Self-Contained Underwater Breathing Apparatus, is a popular method for exploring the underwater world.

SCUBA equipment was invented by Jacques-Yves Cousteau, a Frenchman, in 1943.

Fact
29

When divers submerge in the ocean, they experience weightlessness, similar to astronauts in space.

Astronauts learn to scuba dive at the beginning of their astronaut training to acclimatise themselves to the weightlessness they will encounter when walking in space.

Fact

30

The ocean world is an 'alien' place for human life. It is cold, dark, lacks oxygen and pressure builds to dangerous levels the deeper you go.

It is not possible to fully explore the vast oceans by just walking in from the beach. Even with a mask and snorkel, a swimmer can only explore a few metres below the surface before needing to return to the surface to breathe oxygen.

Fact

31

Humans use SCUBA equipment which includes fins, masks, weights, buoyancy aids, wetsuits and breathing apparatus to stay alive underwater.

Divers take a tank of compressed air (not oxygen) underwater.

Fact

32

Recreational divers generally do not descend beyond depths of 30-40 metres as the pressure on their lungs below that depth becomes too intense for the human body to handle.

To supply oxygen during diving, scuba divers carry a tank of compressed air on their backs. However, it's important to note that oxygen becomes toxic to humans at depths of 55-60 metres below the surface.

Fact

33

The marine environment is natural and houses predators and prey. Underwater exploration to discover marine life is not like visiting a zoo.

Caution is necessary as dangerous animals are not kept in cages. Although many people are afraid of sharks, these creatures aren't always harmful. Luckily, the reef shark being photographed, isn't dangerous to humans.

Fact
34

Humans need to use submersibles to explore the deep oceans.

Submersibles are 'pressurised' so anyone sitting inside is protected from the high water pressure outside in the ocean.

Fact

35

Just as we have different environments on land, such as forests, lakes, deserts, and polar regions, we also have diverse environments in the oceans.

For example, there are smaller habitats like rock pools located in the tidal areas along the coastline. Children are often thrilled to explore beaches that have rock pools because they offer a chance to discover and learn new things.

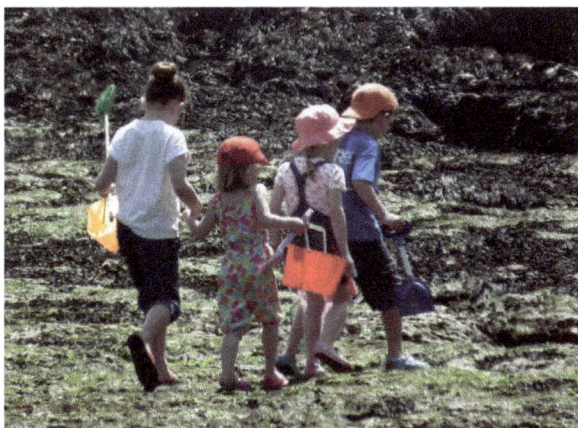

Fact

36

Coral reefs cover only 0.25% of the ocean area, but they are home to 25% of all marine animals. Tropical coral reefs are found near the equator, while temperate coral reefs exist in colder waters.

Tropical coral reefs exist in warm waters near the equator, while temperate corals are found in cooler waters. Coral life does not thrive in polar regions due to low temperatures.

Fact

As you journey across the vast ocean on a ship, you'll be surrounded by blue waters that are home to a magnificent number of aquatic creatures.

Although many of these creatures are not visible to travellers from the ship, you might catch a glimpse of dolphins, whales, or turtles when they surface to breathe. While fish usually stay underwater, you may witness a group of flying fish leaping out of the water as they try to escape from their predators.

Fact

38

The Arctic and Antarctic Oceans have freezing temperatures that cause surface water to freeze during winter.

The world ocean is home to unique creatures like the Greenland shark that dives deep for food and the cold-water cod fish that uses a biological anti-freeze in its blood to survive the freezing climate.

Fact
39

When a ship sinks to the sea bed, it can become an 'artificial' reef. It eventually becomes encrusted with coral as individual polyps inhabit the wreck over time.

A wide variety of organisms live on artificial coral reefs, which provide significant shelter for many coral species.

Fact
40

Seagrass is the only plant in the ocean. Seagrass uses photosynthesis just like plants on land.

Meadows of seagrass grow in shallow waters throughout the world. It is crucial to protect seagrass as it is responsible for releasing up to 10% of all the oxygen in the Earth's atmosphere.

Fact

41

Seagrass and seaweed are two distinctly different organisms. Seagrass is a plant, while seaweed is an algae.

Both seagrass and seaweed use the process of photosynthesis to generate a) oxygen we breathe and b) food (glucose) we eat.

Fact

42

Plankton is a microscopic type of algae that floats in the ocean and also produces oxygen through photosynthesis.

Seaweed and plankton are responsible for producing 70-80% of all the oxygen in the Earth's atmosphere, which is a staggering 330 billion tons. The oceans play a crucial role in sustaining life on our planet.

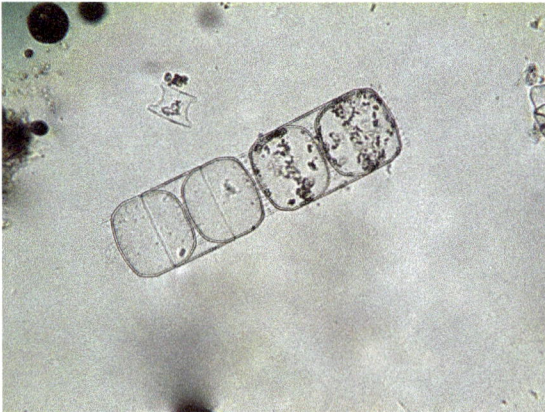

Fact

43

Photosynthesis is considered to be the most important chemical reaction on the planet.

Light from the sun reacts with CO_2 and water and uses the chemical chlorophyll. Photosynthesis makes oxygen and carbohydrates for life on Earth.

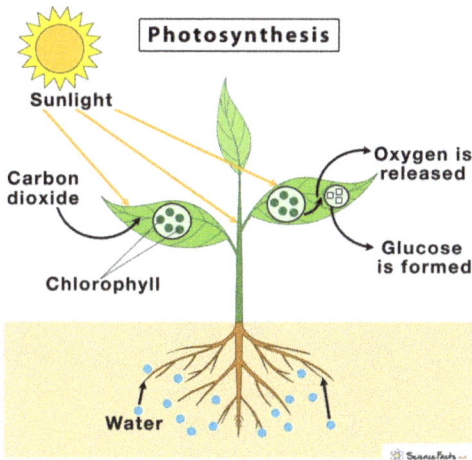

Photosynthesis

Sunlight

Carbon dioxide

Chlorophyll

Oxygen is released

Glucose is formed

Water

Fact

44

Everyone knows about plastic in the oceans and have seen horrific photographs of ocean creatures being entangled in fishing nets.

We must implement zero plastic policies on land to prevent plastic pollution in oceans. Plastic is only one of the many problems humans have caused in the marine environment.

OCEAN POLLUTION
Plastic
Sewage
Fishing / Overfishing
Oil Pollution
Oceans overheating
Oceans turning acidic

Fact

45

The oceans are known as carbon 'sinks' because they absorb carbon dioxide (CO_2) from the atmosphere.

For millions of years, the oceans have acted as a natural balance for the Earth's atmosphere. They absorb CO_2 and release oxygen (O_2).

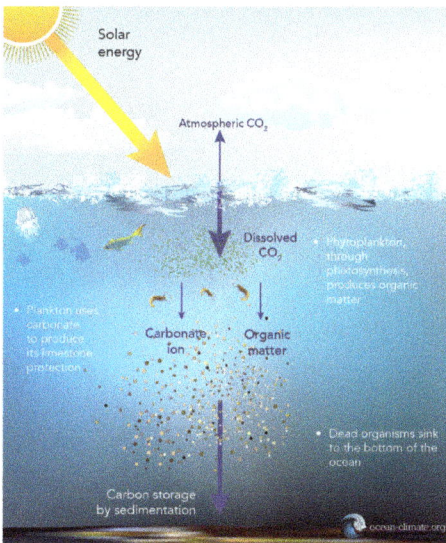

Biological carbon pump

Fact
46

As the ocean absorbs more CO_2, it creates higher levels of carbonic acid.

This severe ocean acidification is causing devastating effects on marine life, including the dissolving of corals and crustacean shells due to increased acidity of the ocean water.

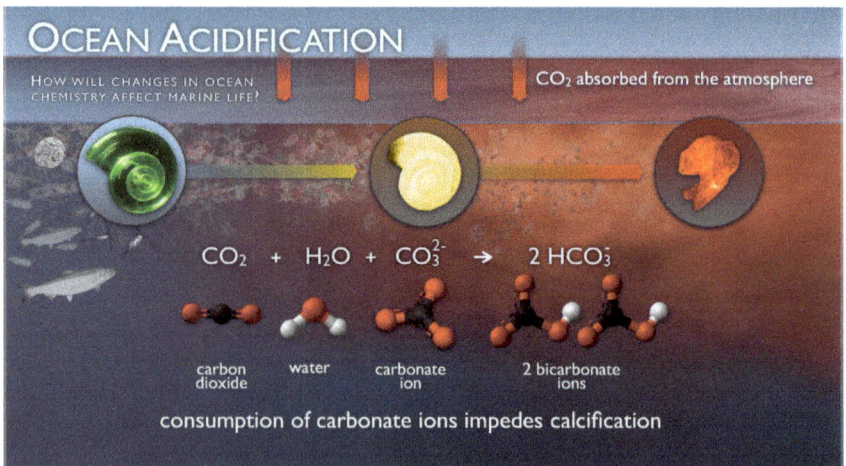

OCEAN ACIDIFICATION

HOW WILL CHANGES IN OCEAN CHEMISTRY AFFECT MARINE LIFE?

CO_2 absorbed from the atmosphere

$$CO_2 + H_2O + CO_3^{2-} \rightarrow 2\ HCO_3^-$$

carbon dioxide   water   carbonate ion   2 bicarbonate ions

consumption of carbonate ions impedes calcification

Fact

47

The Pacific currents have created massive rubbish patches in the world's largest ocean, containing an estimated 1.8 trillion pieces of plastic waste.

Boyan Slat, a young Dutchman, is famous for his efforts to clean up plastic waste in the Pacific Ocean. Let's do everything we can to prevent plastics from polluting our oceans.

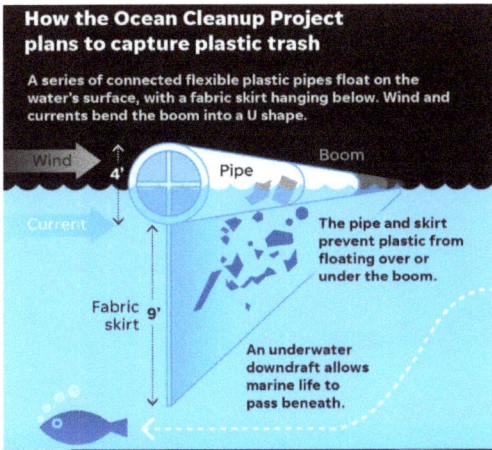

How the Ocean Cleanup Project plans to capture plastic trash

A series of connected flexible plastic pipes float on the water's surface, with a fabric skirt hanging below. Wind and currents bend the boom into a U shape.

Wind

4'

Pipe

Boom

Current

The pipe and skirt prevent plastic from floating over or under the boom.

Fabric skirt 9'

An underwater downdraft allows marine life to pass beneath.

Fact
48

Boyan Slat has expanded his Ocean CleanUp project to include collecting rubbish from rivers.

'River CleanUp' is his latest project. He has designed boats that collect rubbish on a conveyor belt as they travel up rivers away from the oceans. These boats can collect 110,000 kgs of trash from rivers every day, preventing it from entering the ocean.

Fact

49

Scientists discover new ocean creatures and learn more about known ones every day.

Sponges are thought to be among the oldest creatures to inhabit the oceans; however, it wasn't until recently that scientists discovered sponges contain a chemical that may hold the key to curing cancer.

Fact

50

Scientists studying the ocean inform us of its importance to all life on Earth.

It's great news to hear about projects where communities are taking care of the ocean environment. It means it's not only ocean scientists who are working towards ocean conservation, but every one of us can contribute in small ways or by volunteering in groups to collect rubbish or plant more seagrass to improve the ocean's health. There's loads of work we can all do.

Glossary

Earth and Ocean

1. Earth from Space
2. Five oceans – the World Ocean
3. The Oceans cover 70% of the surface area of Earth
4. What s the difference between 'oceans' and 'seas'.

Exploring the oceans

5. HMS Challenger
6. Exploring the deepest part of the oceans.
7. Trenches formed by tectonic plates.
8. Mariana Trench
9. First manned exploration of deep sea trench
10. The descent of 'Trieste'
11. 2010 – James Cameron
12. High tech submersibles

Physical Conditions

13. Salt water
14. Surface Temperature
15. The deeper, the colder
16. Water is a limited resource
17. Freshwater from rain
18. Water Cycle
19. Oxygen in atmosphere and oceans
20. Sea water separates colours of light
21. Sun provides oceans with heat and light
22. Earth is not a perfect sphere.

23. Dive Time
24. Underwater profile of oceans.
25. Wet suits
26. Bioluminescence
27. Epipelagic zone

Scuba Diving

28. Scuba equipment
29. Weightlessness
30. Alien World
31. Temperate Waters
32. Pressure
33. Predators and Prey
34. Icy waters, polar bears and penguins

Ocean environments

35. Rock Pools
36. Coral Reefs
37. Blue waters
38. Arctic and Antarctic
39. Artificial Reefs
40. Seagrass is a plant
41. Seaweed is an algae
42. Microscopic plankton
43. Photosynthesis

Why we need healthy oceans

44. Plastic pollution
45. Carbon sink
46. CO_2 absorption
47. Ocean CleanUp
48. River CleanUp
49. Discovery of new ocean creatures
50. Studying the ocean.

The Water Cycle Stories

There are six ways for water droplets to travel back to the ocean.

Story A. **Domestic Water**

I am inside the rain which has been collected.
I am now in a water collection point for household water.
I travel down a tap into a house.
I am used in a bath before a child's bedtime.
I get released down the plug hole into the water disposal system.
I travel along pipes and am released back into the Ocean.

Story B. **Run-Off**

I am inside the rain which has fallen on a mountain side.
I reach a stream and flow down to a river.
The river flows down to the Ocean and I am released into the Ocean.

Story C. **Ground Water**

I am inside the rain which falls on a field. I get soaked down under the earth:
- sometimes near the surface (go to Story E) or
sometimes deep underground. (go to Story D)
I eventually end up back in the Oceans.

Story D. Deep Underground

I am taken deep under the surface and fall into spaces between the rocks. These spaces can store water for ages.
I think I might be here for some time before I eventually get returned to the cycle and end up in the Ocean again.

Story E. Transpiration

The Ground Water has left me near the surface, under a tree. The tree's roots pull me up, through the inside of the tree to the leaves.
I help the leaves to make glucose and oxygen (photosynthesis)
The water not needed for photosynthesis is released from the leaves into the air as **transpiration.**
I get caught up in a cloud and travel around the water cycle again, and eventually end up back in the Ocean

Story F. **Respiration**

I find myself under the grass.
The roots of the grass pull me up into the blades of the grass.
A cow comes along and eats me.
I get released when the cow breathes out. **Respiration.**
I get caught up in a cloud, travel around the water cycle again, and eventually end up back in the Ocean.

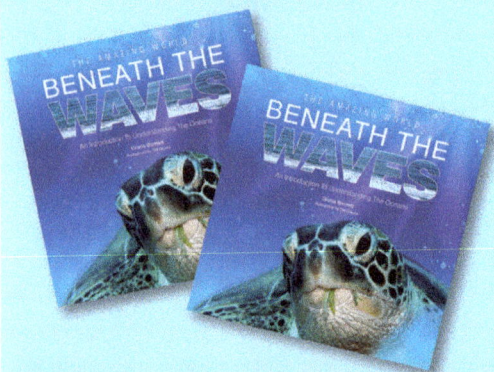

Gloria Barnett is an award-winning author with a passion for science, particularly in ocean studies and climate change. Her extensive knowledge and expertise in these fields make her an exceptional writer for all age groups.

Gloria's love for the natural world is infectious. Her 30 years of experience exploring the world's oceans as a master scuba diver, sailor, and underwater videographer has given her a practical understanding of the sea and its inhabitants.

She has been a strong advocate for conservation for many years and written a range of books, including non-fiction guides on oceans and climate change, as well as children's fiction for 3-6 and 8-13-year-olds.

www.barnettauthor.co.uk.

Published in 2024

An imprint from
Footprint to the Future
Publishers of resources to help understanding
of Planet Earth.
165 London Road Temple Ewell, Kent, CT16 3DA

A CIP record for this title is available from the British Library

ISBN 978-1-7393084-2-1

Book Design: www.amberdesigns.com

Published by: www.footprinttothefuture.co.uk

IMAGE CREDITS/FACT NUMBERS

Shutterstock	4,17,19	C.Barnett	39,49
NASA	1,6,21,29	Encyclopedia Britannica	22
Tiki Graves	2,3,7,24	Blue Marine Foundation	25
Royal Naval Museum Greenwich	5	A. Georgetti	33
Creative Commons	8,12,34,43	R.Stonehouse	36
NOAA	9,10,14,15,16,26,46	C.Best	42
National Geographic	11	oceanclimate.org	45
WHOI	27	Ocean CleanUp	47,48
Adobe Stock	13,18,23,30,38,40,41	Communities for Seas, WWF	50
G.Barnett	20,28,31,32,35,37,44